Copyright © 2025
Scott L Bell

eBook 978-1-7643855-0-3
paperback 978-1-7643855-1-0
hardcover 978-1-7643855-2-7

All Rights Reserved. Any unauthorized reprint or use of this material is strictly prohibited. No part of this book may be reproduced or transmitted in any form or by any means, electronic or mechanical, including photocopying, recording, or by any information storage and retrieval system without express written permission from the author.

All reasonable attempts have been made to verify the accuracy of the information provided in this publication. Nevertheless, the author assumes no responsibility for any errors and/or omissions.

THE COLOUR GREY

A Testament of Survival and Silence.

A collection of Poems
By Scott Bell

Acknowledgements

I acknowledge everything and nothing—God and the Devil, light and dark, hope and despair. I acknowledge the hands that built me, and the hands that broke me. The voices that silenced, and the voices that screamed. I acknowledge the world—indifferent, unyielding. And I acknowledge myself: the witness to it all.

Dedication

To the weeds in the garden bed: the world may curse our names, but still we rise—stubborn and green—outgrowing every fragile bloom. Our beauty is not in petals, but in the quiet truth of resilience.

Author

Scott Bell's work is rooted in raw honesty, exploring the grey spaces between trauma and resilience, despair and hope.
Contact: scott.lewis.bell@gmail.com

Contents

Act I: Origin   5
Grey is the Colour of Inheritance   7
Grey is the Colour of the Door   9
Grey is the Colour of Smoke   11

Act II: Rupture   13
Grey is the Colour of the Jacket   15
Grey is the Colour of Stone   17
Grey is the Colour of Touch   19
Grey is the Colour of Devotion   22
Grey is the Colour of Death   25
Grey is the Colour of Hate   28

Act III: Endurance   31
Grey is the Colour of Attachment   33
Grey is the Colour of Being Seen   37
Grey is the Colour of Desire   39
Grey is the Colour of the End   41
Grey is the Colour of Hunger   43
Grey is the Colour of Mind   45

Act IV: Renewal   47
Grey is the Colour of Letting Go   49
Grey is the Colour of Hope   50
Grey is the Colour of Routine   52
Grey is the Colour of Mountains   54
Grey is the Colour of Balance   58

Act V: Revelation   60

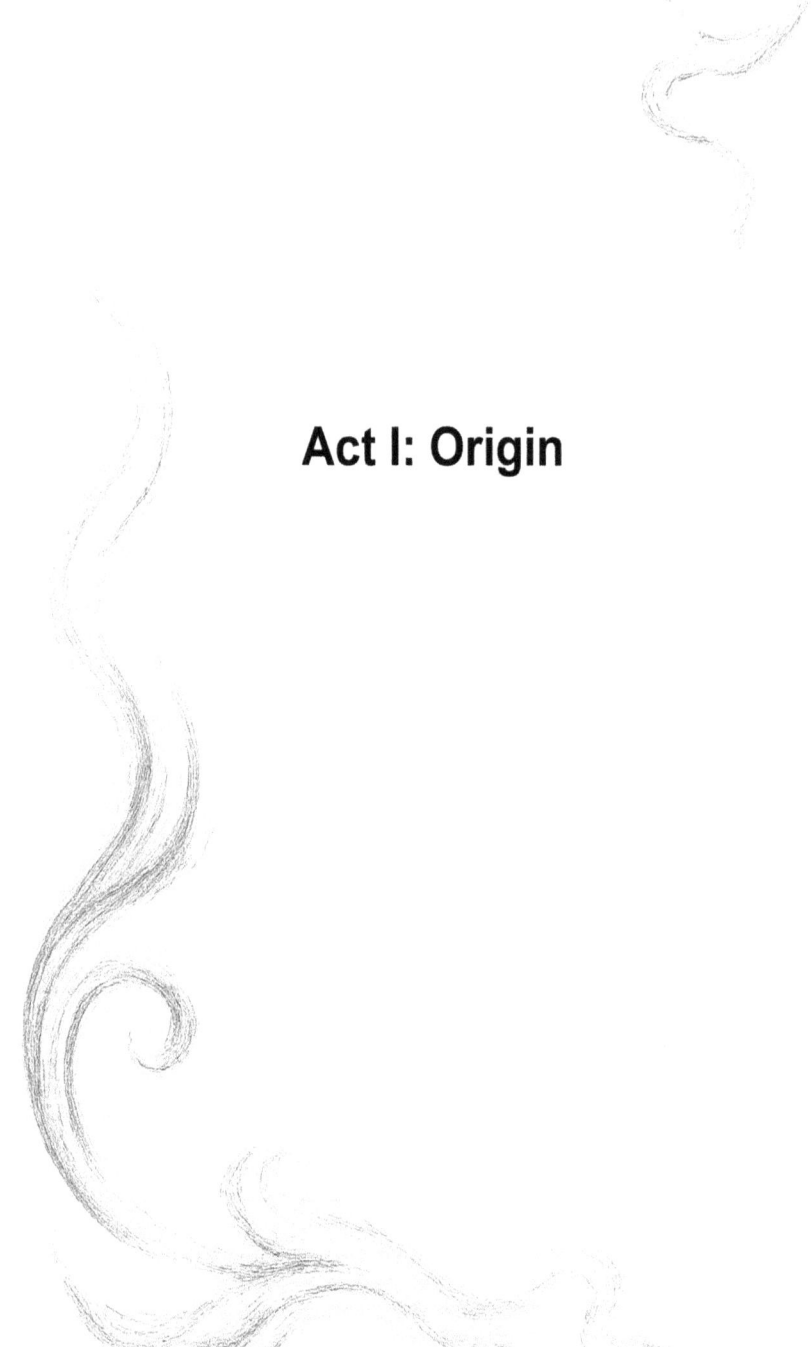

Act I: Origin

Grey is the Colour of Inheritance

Still, grey is the colour I call friend.
It speaks neither of light nor of darkness,
only of itself.

Encircled, I begin to shake.
Has it always been this way?
Did I mistake warmth
for stone echoing back?

Perhaps I learned to love the void—
its indifference,
its refusal to care.

I am the child of grey.
I thrived in violence.
I endured the touch I did not want.
I found pleasure in the devil.
I went where shadows hid.

And yet what is grey but excuse,
a sky that forgets its own mouth.
No one blesses a grey morning,
yet it carries rain,
and rain, bitter or kind,
still feeds the root.

Paradox, then—
no curse, no blessing.
A gift without ceremony.
Nothing to announce,
nothing to refuse.

Trapped, with land to walk.
Free, with lines already drawn.
Loved, with conditions that do not move.

This is my inheritance:
the quiet between extremes,
the dull hum of being.

Grey companion.
Grey captor.
Grey that will not flatter—
ash on the tongue
that still tastes of rain.

Grey is the Colour of the Door

Mint skirting lined the hall,
eggshell faces practiced smiles for strangers.
A gallery of borrowed love.

The bathroom reeked of chemicals,
cheap perfume and disinfectant prayers.
A blue toilet crouched
on its furred island.
The air remembered more than I could name.

A door shut.
A child balanced on porcelain,
feet dangling.
The light—
always out of reach.

Knock.
A small reply.
Knock again, sharper.
The frame filled with shadow.

Too large.
Too near.
The latch sealed the silence.

Touch that was not touch,
a tongue like theft.
The body betrayed.
Tears slid unnoticed;
the floor received them.

Cloth lifted from linoleum,
the child clothed again
but not covered.

The hallway stretched eternal,
mint boards a blur,
each step echoing—
useless, useless.

Outside, beneath the mailbox, a thought:
Can I be folded into an envelope,
stamped,
sent elsewhere?

The sky hung low,
grey and without answer,
pressing itself to the earth
like a hand that would not lift.

Grey is the Colour of Smoke

When smoke leaves the body, it drifts grey.
Each breath a quiet surrender,
each exhale carrying wounds
too heavy to speak.

I chased numbness
as if silence could cradle me.
She taught me to follow the smoke—
her beauty a lantern,
her voice water,
her arms the only home I knew.

The ritual was careful:
steady hand, steady flame,
foil trembling with heat.
They warned it was the end,
the indulgence of the damned.
But I never belonged to their world.

I thought the smoke would be black,
as dark as the stone itself,
but it rose grey, soft.
I felt nothing,
I felt everything,
and in that blur

I called it beautiful.

I returned again and again,
until the morning I woke
and she did not.

Her face was blue,
her skin cold,
and no one heard me cry.

At the funeral, photographs
invented a daughter
who wanted to sew dresses,
but was remembered as ruin.

I knew the truth:
her father, the wolf
draped in the skin of the pious.

Still the smoke rises,
grey, unrelenting,
lingering in the lungs of memory—
a prayer for her,
a requiem for love,
a ruin I cannot release.

Act II: Rupture

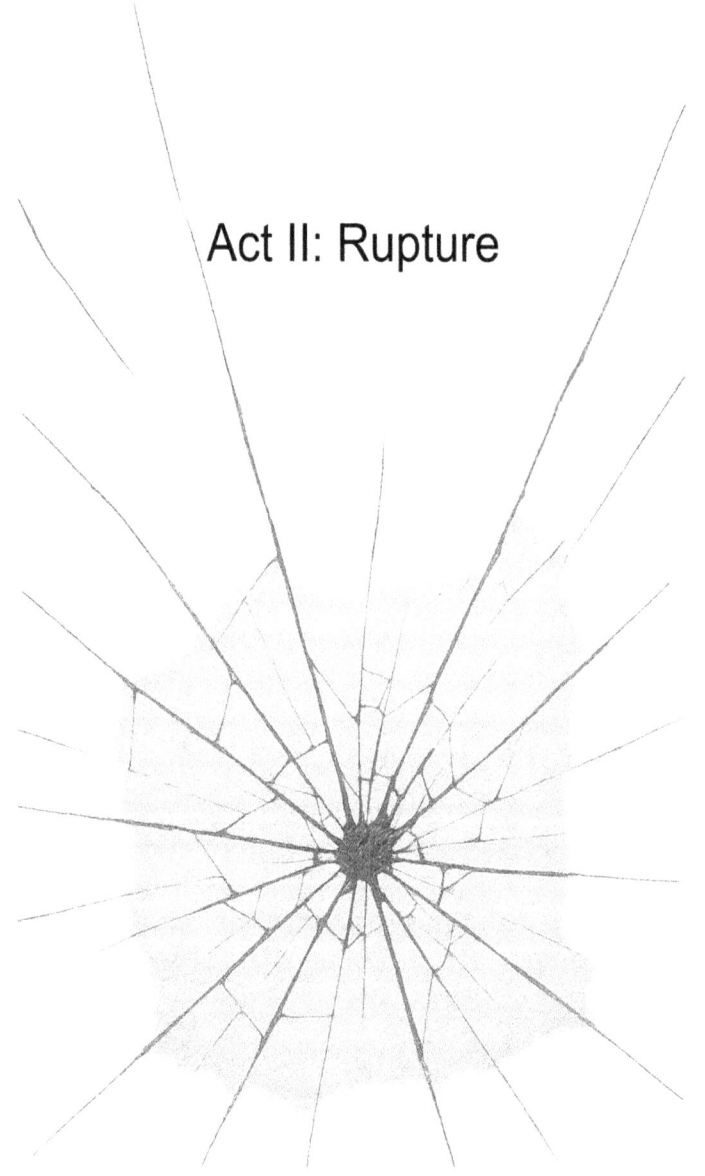

Grey is the Colour of the Jacket

Grey was the jacket he wore—
not soldier's pride,
but a relic from some forgotten shop,
its threads stinking of beer and smoke.

I called him Father,
longed for Dad.
I wanted the weight of his gaze,
to feel like blood,
not shadow.

But love was a wage
others earned by existing.
I was the baggage—
the step-son trailing
behind a waitress
who traded her body for four walls.

"Dad, can you be my dad?"
"No. Yours is out there—
a madman, a ghost."

So I became weight.
Weight turned inconvenience.
Inconvenience grew teeth.

His fists wrote the law:
fear is control,
fear makes men,
fear bleeds the art from boys
who dare to sing or draw.

And she—
the silent witness—
never spoke.

So I believed the silence:
I am bad.
I am unworthy.

But all beaten dogs learn.
When they bite, it is betrayal.
When they defend, it is their fault.
A dog struck may still cower,
but when it bares its teeth
the night opens,
and it is cast into it.

Grey is the Colour of Stone

Grey is not sorrow,
but teacher—
the hue of patience,
the fuel that keeps
a quiet fire warm.

I have learned to dwell in it,
content, even proud.

Grey is the stone of my castle.
Its walls rise against the horizon,
seen by any who wander near.
Yes, the stones crumble in places,
yes, secrets are kept within—
but still it stands,
perfect in its fractures.

I once believed anger was medicine,
a bitter draught for others to drink.
But it poisoned only me.

I was different,
uncelebrated,
outcast.
And in that exile

I found my pride.

A wise man once said:
be a lamp in your own darkness.

I say:
be the foundation.
Build your empires,
stone by stone,
grey and strong,
proud and eternal.

Grey is the Colour of Touch

Before thought was born,
before language sharpened itself into blade,
creatures reached for one another—
their hands knowing more than their minds.

Touch is the hunger I carry,
a beautiful ache,
yet I recoil from the hands of many.
I have known unwanted touch;
its memory claws me still.

Anger rises from the marrow.
The body hardens into weapon.

False prophets land on my shore,
hands outstretched like salvation.
But their offerings are hollow—
not intimacy, only lust,
not closeness, only urgency.

Their altars crumble.
Their sermons end in silence.
I am left with echoes in my skin.

The most painful touch?

The one without meaning—
a hand that pretends,
a hand that lies.
Obligation pressed to skin
is a wound that does not close.

How long must longing endure?
How long must denial rot?
I ache for a chosen touch—
not duty, not habit,
but fire, worship, need.

So I stand on an island
beneath a sky of endless grey.
I build my lighthouse,
dress it in beauty.
Its beam stretches across the sea,
but it draws only poor ships,
laden with hollow cargo.

At its foot, my dog keeps vigil—
faithful, unyielding,
driving the strangers away,
yet leaving me waiting
for the ship brave enough
to silence his growl.

When will I be touched—
not as duty,
not as habit,
but as choice,
as fire,
as need?

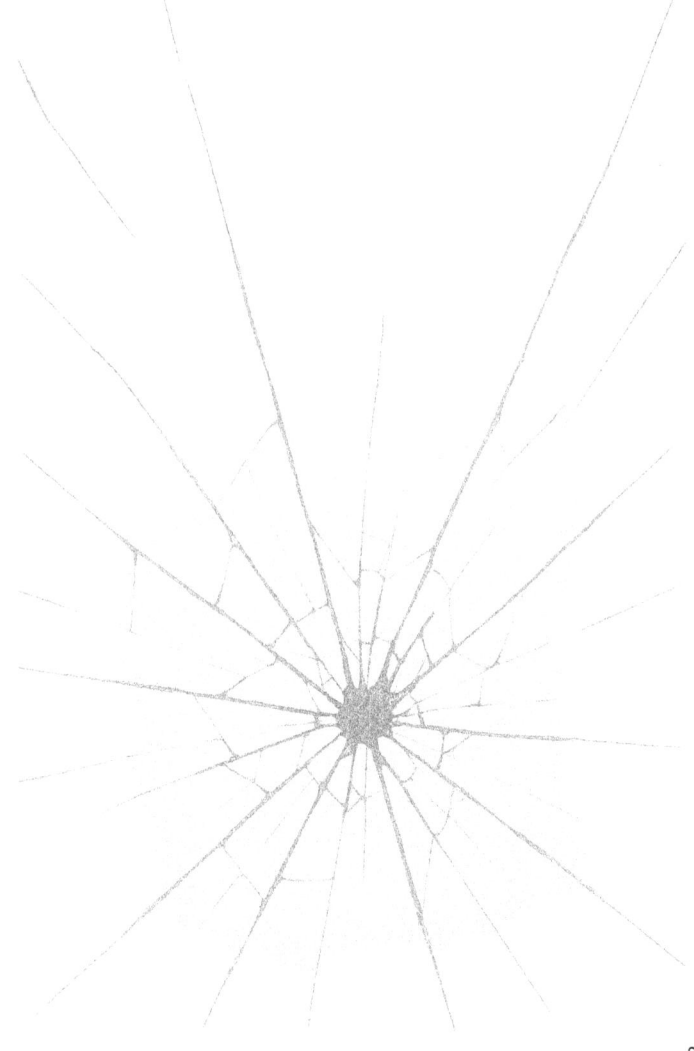

Grey is the Colour of Devotion

Grey is the colour of devotion.
Not the flare of beginnings,
not the ash of endings—
but the steady hum of staying.

Years have passed.
I stood, wallet in hand,
offering presence as currency:
discipline, intention, care.
I built with these.
Still, the diamond cracked.

There is remorse,
regret tempered by memory.
Love deserves its eulogy.
But resentment clings like smoke.

She was right:
time is not infinite.
Time is currency too.

Samsara—
the monks named it well.
This cycle:
devotion met with silence,

effort lost in the churn.

Again I stand in wasted worship.
My tenderness,
a cloak turned invisible.
My hand, once extended,
hangs by my side.

A father, they say I will be.
Yet I wait in the shadows,
obedient,
like a loyal dog
outside the door of his own home.

Father's Day—
a quiet house,
no honour,
only foundations
turning back to sand.

Is this karma,
or the weight of being unseen
too many times?

I no longer burn.
Even anger curls into itself.

Apathy rocks me,
ferrying me always
to the island of grey.

Grey is the Colour of Death

Grey is the colour of death.
Nights stretched thin,
each second clutched
as though it might stay.
But time marches on,
indifferent, unrelenting.

Sometimes I beg it to pause,
to let me hold the fragments.
But it does not pause.
It only reminds me:
no beginning without end,
no end without beginning.

Am I hopeful,
or simply devastated?

I once took my life—twice—
and failed.
Was it cruelty,
or disguise of opportunity?
Even now I wander
through the corridors of that choice.

Now fate has spoken.

The card of death lies on the table.
What is dying?
What is living?
The fog holds the answers back.

I am angry.
I hate the loss of control.
I want the helm,
but the world denies me.

They say we cannot command the wind,
only adjust the sails.
But I ask: to where?
To the horizon unknown?
To shores once abandoned?
Or straight into the jaws of ruin?

Blind optimism is for fools.
Negativity for the weak.
It simply is.

And when death comes, we must choose:
to stand tall, surrender with dignity,
to be reborn—
or thrash against the reaper's hand,
dragged screaming into endless dark.

The clock ticks.
The calendar turns.
The sky shifts overhead.

My death is coming.
Certain. Silent. Unstoppable.

But what is dying?
Even that,
I do not know.

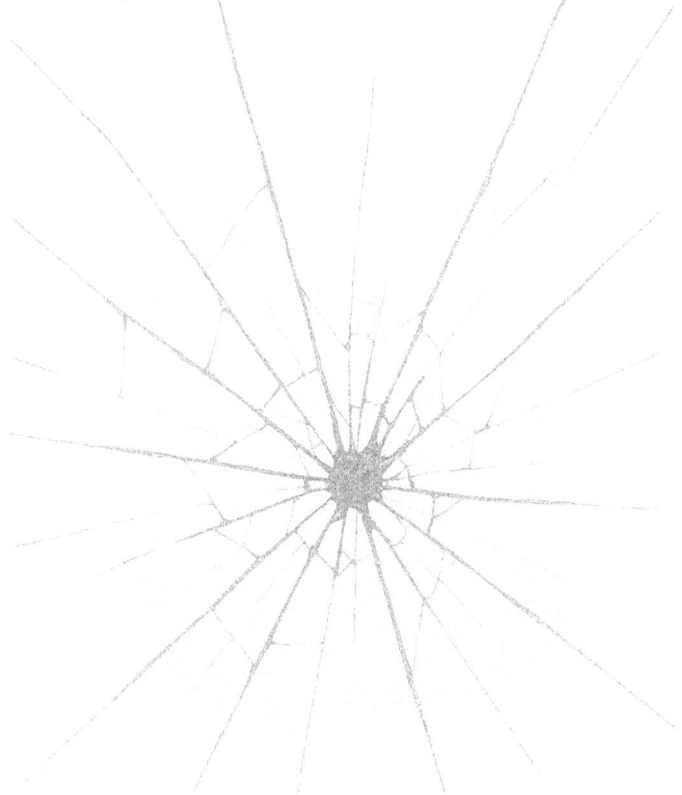

Grey is the Colour of Hate

Not red — too brief.
Not black — too final.
Grey waits.
Patient.
Quiet.
It asks for nothing,
except that you stop pretending.

It seeps in slowly —
through tired thoughts,
through clenched hands,
through sleepless nights.
It does not shout.
It hums,
low and constant,
an engine that will not switch off.

For a time I believed I needed it.
Grey gave me reason
when reason felt pointless.
It filled hollow spaces
where warmth had died.
It told me I was strong
because nothing could hurt me.
And I believed it.

But hate hurts.
It costs everything to keep alive.
You feed a fire
that gives nothing back.
It burns only what is inside you,
and the smoke blinds you to all else.

Still —
I like its sharpness.
It wakes me.
It drives me.
But I hate its grip —
how it owns me,
how it makes breathing
an excuse not to heal.

There is no peace in it.
No comfort.
No joy.
Only the rhythm of anger
pretending to be purpose.

And when the silence comes,
when the rage runs dry,
I feel the weight.
I cannot remember who I was

before grey settled in my bones.

Am I the only one to blame?
Or is there empathy too?
Because hate is not born of nothing.
It grows from wounds,
from love turned bitter,
from promises undone.

Perhaps grey is not absence,
but overflow —
too many colours bleeding together:
love, loss, fear, anger —
a palette blurred
until nothing is clear.

That is why it feels familiar.
Because hate is not the end of feeling.
It is what remains
when you cannot stop feeling,
but do not know how to forgive.

Act III: Endurance

Grey is the Colour of Attachment

There is hope in solitary confinement.
I paint the walls with my own colours,
choose the light that softens or hardens the stone.
Safe in silence,
safe where no one can wound me.

Outside the door,
barbecues and children screaming,
plastic smiles traded like currency.
Connection as ritual,
connection as performance.

Once, my family told me football was god.
But I hid in trees,
in a cubby made of scraps,
listening to a cassette of 1992's anthems
until the batteries bled out.
I begged for more life.
I wanted to sing,
to write,
but song was weakness,
and weakness was shame.

Already, I was learning disconnection,
learning to bury colour.

When I let them in,
I left gravestones scattered along the road,
each carved with a piece of my heart.
I hate them for it—
their hands teaching me pain.

I loved once,
truly loved.
I wrapped myself around her warmth,
showed her colour.
She tore me open.
I wandered schoolyards,
streets without anchor,
alive only with the sharp taste of pain.

Pain can be beautiful—
it proves you are not stone.
But its weight drags, and drags.

Years became a litany of heartbreak.
So I closed.
I vowed my heart would never be touched again.
In that vow I grew mysterious.
People begged to know me.
The more they begged,
the more I sealed the veil.

On rare occasions,
when I showed a sliver of colour,
they called me weak,
needy,
too much.

So I learned to lie.
Safer to fold truth away—
though lies cut like hidden blades.

I am not for the faint of heart.
I carry weights that would splinter others.
I hold them in full acceptance
because I know rejection's sting.

But do not ask me to share in return.
I will not.
I cannot.

Stoic.
Silent.
Hidden.

Life is safer this way.
I walk alone, keeping control—
because to hand someone the truth of me

is to give them the blade
that could break my heart.

Grey is the Colour of Being Seen

I hibernate within myself,
aged in spirit,
my quest to be seen
turning to dust in my hands.

Among the crowd I walk armoured,
defensive,
guarding the fragile brand of who I am.

Too complex.
Too emotional.
Too selfish.
Too much.

I beg them to see me
before I speak—
an unfair demand.

Walls rise.
Anger stains my face.
You will not see me.
You will not accept me.
You will not know me.

And yet—

I judge you for not seeing
what I refuse to reveal.
We are blind together.
And that is my fault.

Beneath the mask,
I only long to be embraced,
to be understood,
to be seen.

Still, I recoil.
To be seen frightens me.
I push away what I crave.
The cycle begins again.

When will I take responsibility—
open myself
and allow many eyes
to truly meet me?

Or will I linger in shadow,
calling out:

See me.
Don't see me.
See me.
Stay blind.

Grey is the Colour of Desire

Every day,
I think of you.

Leave me,
or take me.

I run from you in every direction,
but every road bends back
to your shadow.

I build my week
around the moments
I might see you.
The rest I spend in waiting,
urging the hours to die
so two minutes of breath
might pass between us.

I am angry—
angry at the ritual of waiting,
angry at being robbed
of what I crave.

I am caged in my own hunger,
hands trembling to touch

but never allowed.

You have become a habit,
a wound I keep reopening.

Work is you.
Life is you.
Love is you.
I wake for you
and hold nothing
but the hope of you.

I hate you.
I love you.

Grey is the Colour of the End

Can you see the curtain?
It hangs heavier than before,
velvet wet with years of dust.
The show is ending.
Puppets once full of life
slacken in their strings.

The crowd grows restless,
faces turning to the exit.
Reviews will hit the papers by midnight,
ink still warm.

The song rises to its last crescendo,
a hollow cathedral of sound.
Reverb rings the final note—
a note that does not return.

Applause trickles in,
not joy,
but obligation.

The stage is littered with puppets,
painted eyes staring into nothing.
They are finished.
No breath left.

The crowd departs.
The hall empties.
Only dust remains,
falling like slow snow.

The noose is tied.
The letters written.
The candle sighs itself out.

The tour is over.
The show can only be remembered.

The puppeteer lingers
in the ghost-light of the stage,
rows of empty seats before him,
a priest at an abandoned altar.

The wooden chair creaks.
The beam groans.
The theatre exhales.

Dust practices
its slow applause.

Grey is the Colour of Hunger

I reach for what no longer reaches back.
The connection I bled for
slips through my hands like water,
mocking my thirst.

I am desperate.
Not gentle, not patient—
desperate.

The ache of her absence
gnaws against my ribs,
a void that memory cannot fill.

I loved being wanted,
loved being necessary.
Her hunger crowned me with meaning.
Now the crown is gone,
and I stand stripped,
a kingdom in ashes.

Something in me snarls for more.
I crave new skin,
a stranger's warmth,
to taste the unfamiliar,
to baptize myself in lust

until the anger cools
and the craving quiets.

Grey is the colour of loss.
Grey is the colour of wanting.
Grey is the colour of a beast unchained,
searching for anything
to replace the wound.

Grey is the color of mind

a sky without sun,
a winter without thaw.

For years I have watched myself erode,
slipping between shadows of who I was.
Some mornings I rise almost whole,
others I whimper,
a soaked dog trembling
in the alleyways of thought.

Memory is my traitor and my kin—
its hands both cradle and choke.
Each day reshapes itself,
a labyrinth with no exit.
Nightmares slip in like thieves,
whispering secrets
only the broken can understand.

Doom rises—
a black tide, unstoppable,
the heart stutters,
the mind freezes,
and I fracture into silence.

The tide drags me deeper,

deeper still,
and I drown
in its static stillness.
Once I have grown,
all I can do is fade.

Why can't I be normal?
What curse was carved
into my bones
that I wake dreading daylight
and beg for night
only to be hunted by my dreams?

Still—
one pill after another,
one flail from moment to moment—
this, perhaps,
is the closest thing to living
I will ever know.

Act IV: Renewal

Grey is the Colour of Letting Go

Grey is the colour of letting go.
To release you is to release myself—
a severing of shadow from body,
a quiet undoing of all that held me still.

No longer do I wait for our dawn.
The mornings come without your name,
and though the silence trembles,
I breathe in its raw simplicity.

Ahead, a horizon opens,
its edge lit with hesitant light.
It carries both promise and pain—
departure as arrival.

The ache lingers,
but it no longer binds.

I step forward, unshackled,
knowing that to let you go
is not only to lose,
but to begin.

Grey is the Colour of Hope

If it all ended—
untold, unsaid,
buried beneath years of rejection
and the gnawing weight of loathing—
would anyone hear it?
Would anyone notice?

The world spins by,
phone in hand,
life reduced to a weary trudge.

Life is pain.
Life is hard.

Yet—
life is beautiful.
For every wound,
I have known wonder.
For every descent,
I found a fragment in the dark.

So I wade through torment,
learning, mourning, growing.
Somehow—
not drowning.

Hope is no gift,
but something forged
when the world withholds mercy.

Scarred and hollow—
these are my truths.
Yet resilience keeps me steady.

The noose whispers,
its voice as familiar as breath.
But not now, my friend.
Not today.

Grey is the Colour of Routine

The day is predicted—
a law no one escapes.
One foot after the other,
one motion living,
the next only watching.

I give the bigger slice away,
my hunger folded into napkins,
pressed flat with good manners.
This is stability—
earned, worn thin,
a love-hate truce with order.

Food on the table,
seasoned with care,
already dissolving
into habit, into need,
into the muscle memory of survival.

Talk stripped bare—
no discovery left,
only the small mercy
of polite rehearsal.

Repeat. Resent. Repeat.
They call it contentment.

An itchy finger waits
inside my jacket—
the fuse, the bomb.
Would it free me,
or forge a darker kind of cage?

A dog roams the same yard for years.
Now the gate swings open.
He stands still.
Ears flicking.
The wind of the road in his nose.
Does he bolt,
or curl on the porch,
nose to tail,
content with the hand that feeds?

To be kept—
or to be free?

The road smells like rain.
No sound but breath
and the slow hinge of the gate.

Grey is the Colour of Mountains

I have lingered for hours
at the foot of this mountain,
circling its base like a shadow
searching for an opening.

I pressed my palms to stone,
pushed until my body frayed.
Now I am empty—
polite in surrender,
too weary to conjure
another try.

It is cruel.
I am sore.
I traded shelter for progress—
and found only rain,
cold on my skin,
mocking my devotion.

How did I arrive here?
Was I mistaken for a mountain goat
when I am only a sloth—
slow, deliberate, miscast in the climb?
A fish scaling a tree?,
lungs burning with borrowed air?

I feel less than.
A cautionary tale.
Unseen.

Or is this what I am meant to believe?
Is the path this steep for everyone?
Do I lack the tools, the discipline,
while the slope softens for others?

No—
this is softness, I tell myself.
Be harder.
Fight more.
Complain less.

I step.
My ankle snaps.
I step again.
I fall face-first.
Mud fills my mouth.
I crawl.
I slide lower.

The mountain hums, indifferent.
Anger burns in my chest.
Tears sting my eyes.

Every breath a chain.

Then—
a flicker in the mist,
a shape between despair and sky.
A rope appears.
Thick. Coarse. Sturdy.
A miracle of texture in my numb hands.
It does not judge,
does not slip.
It burns my palms,
yet holds my weight.

Had I imagined it once?
Dreamed of something to grasp?
Where has it been—
this tether, this grace?
Did I earn it,
or was it waiting all along?

The climb becomes easy.
Stone softens.
The rope pulls, steady as faith,
and like a dream
I did not deserve,
I reach the summit.

I stand at the top in disbelief—
all because of a rope.

I turn to it.

It is you—
the hand I once wished for
at the foot of the mountain.

Grey is the Colour of Balance

It lives between complaint and gratitude,
between the heavy sigh
and the whispered thanks.

Loved, yet used.
Successful, yet broke.
Creative, unheard.
Never alone—
only alone in thought.

Grey is the colour of contradiction.
Trauma in one hand,
a good day in the other.
Light leaking through the cracks,
warmth fading on my skin,
shadow filling them again.

Someone once told me
life is a fight
between chaos and stability.
Lean too far into either,
and the world tilts—
you feel the air slip,
the ground give way beneath your feet.

Grey is the colour of learning to stand still.
Of knowing it is enough
to breathe,
to hurt,
to share,
to let yourself be seen.

Grey does not promise joy,
nor does it condemn to despair.
It hums in the middle—
quiet, steady,
the voice that says:
I am here.

And with that,
I am content
living in grey.

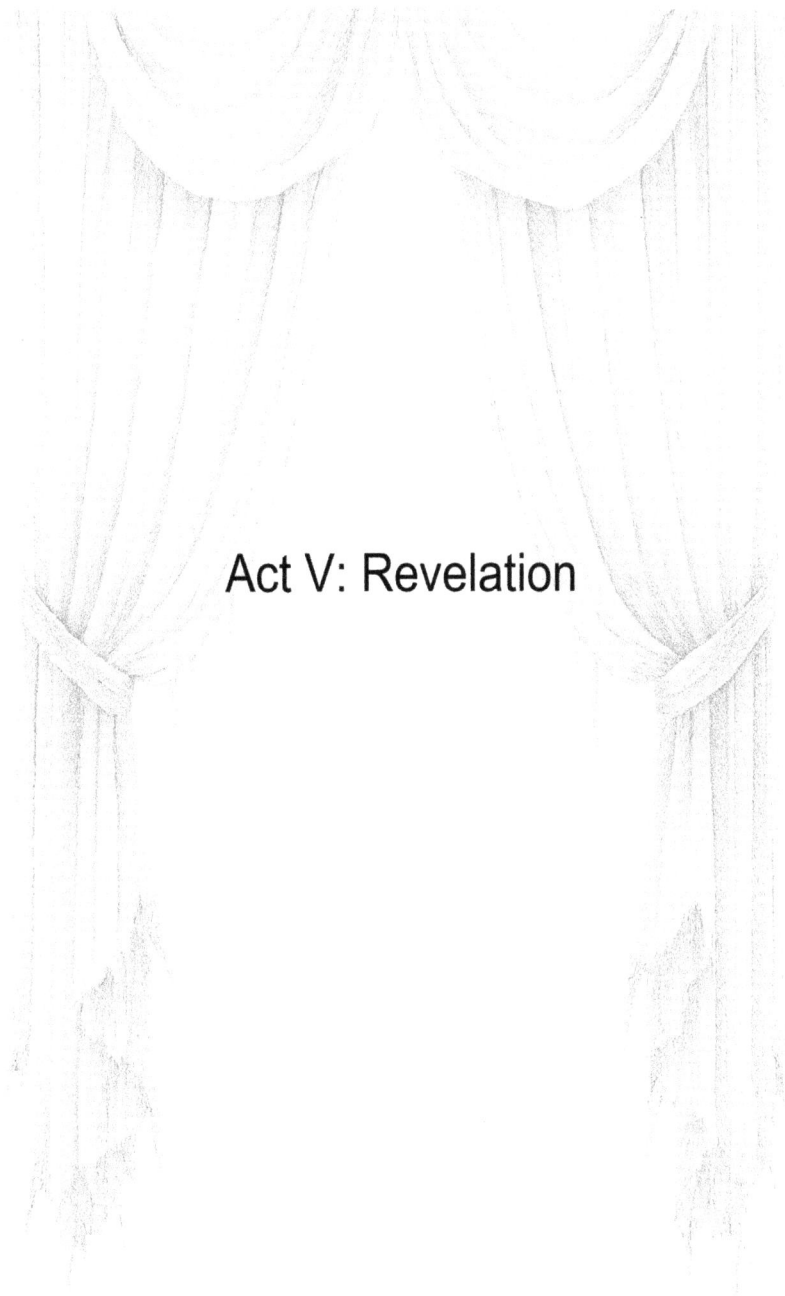

Act V: Revelation

Grey Is the Colour of Revelation

Eternal darkness holds no review,
no memory,
no emotion.

The curtain opens.
I sit—
the only member of an audience
to watch a show I have made.

The stage is chaos.
Between light and dark, the air is grey—
a place where meaning almost forms.
Images scatter,
a thousand random messages,
each stripped of meaning.
Nothing connects—
until a rhythm hums beneath the noise,
a pattern I did not design—
yet know.

The fragments sway,
align,
move as one.

The final message arrives:

Life only exists
as I allow it to exist.
A power so basic,
so unmagical,
that it feels almost holy.

It is not positive.
It is not negative.
It is you—
the piece on the chessboard
without rules,
still bound
by consequence.

Behold—
the last message:

A voice—mine, yet not—
says,
"I do not exist.
Because I am you.
Your mind.
Your decision.
Your choice."

And when darkness returns,

you will sit alone
watching the show
that was your life.

Substance means nothing
without you.

This—
this is how we live in grey

***

If nothing else is remembered of me,
let it be this:
I endured.
I laughed.
I cried.
I loved.
And still I do.

In the true anarchy of stagnation,
I stand —
for you, stranger,
for my solace in you,
and for the refusal
of static failure.

***

A collection of poems that move through
inheritance, devotion, loss, and the quiet truths
of grey. Scott Bell's *The Colour Grey* is a raw
exploration of the spaces between extremes —
where sorrow becomes wisdom, longing shapes
resilience, and devotion outlasts despair.

"Grey, my compannion.
Grey, my captor.
Grey — the colour that tells no lies."

www.ingramcontent.com/pod-product-compliance
Lightning Source LLC
Chambersburg PA
CBHW041302240426
43661CB00010B/994